UK V
Registration

What you need to know – the essential guide for small businesses

James Cooper-Watson

CW01663359

Copyright © 2017 James Cooper-Watson

Author: James Cooper-Watson

Publisher: Hickman.Smyth Publishing

If you have any comments or suggestions for future editions we would love to hear from you, please email us at publishing@hickmansmyth.com

Version 1.0, July 2017

All rights reserved. No part of this book may be reproduced, stored in a retrieval system or transmitted in any form or by any means, electronic, mechanical, photocopying, recording or otherwise without the prior written permission of the Author.

No responsibility for loss occasioned to any person or corporate body acting or refraining to act as a result of reading this book, or any part of this book, can be accepted by the Author or any person connected to them.

Contents

Introduction

Value Added Tax (VAT) is a tax on the sale of goods and services in the UK. Not all goods and services are liable to VAT and not all business need to register for VAT.

This book will explain who **needs** to be VAT Registered and when they should be registered. It will also detail who should consider being VAT registered, even though there is no obligation for them to be.

Who will benefit from this book

If you are running your own business or planning on doing so in the near future, you should read this book. It will explain your obligations from a VAT point of view so that you understand what you should look out for and when you need to take action.

There are also a number of circumstances that may actually make it beneficial to register for VAT before you are legally required to. These scenarios will be explained with the use of real life examples.

CHAPTER 1: Rates of VAT

It is important to understand the different rates of VAT and the goods and services which are charged at each rate. This is because you will need to know which rate(s) would apply to the sale of your goods and services should you need, or want, to become VAT registered.

There are three rates of VAT, which are currently:

Zero rate	0%
Reduced rate	5%
Standard rate	20%

There are also supplies which are exempt from VAT.

If you sell goods exclusive of VAT (i.e. add on VAT) you multiply the value of goods and services by the appropriate rate above to get the VAT inclusive amount, e.g. accountancy fees of £1,000 + VAT = £1,200 including VAT.

If you sell goods inclusive of VAT (so the price you advertise is the price the customer pays) then you multiply the VAT inclusive price by the following fractions to work out the VAT amount:

Reduced rate	1/21
Standard rate	1/6

So, in the accountancy fees above, £1,200 inclusive of VAT, to get the VAT you would do £1,200 x 1/6 = £200.

For a reduced rated item, say your gas at home with a bill of £105, the VAT would be £105 x 1/21 = £5.

Zero rated supplies

Zero rated goods and services are listed in Schedule 8 of the Value Added Tax Act 1994 which can be found in full here:

http://www.legislation.gov.uk/ukpga/1994/23/schedule/8

The different zero rated goods and services are:

Group Number	Goods/Services
1	Food
2	Sewerage service and water
3	Books etc.
4	Talking books for the blind and handicapped and wireless sets for the blind
5	Construction of buildings etc.
6	Protected buildings
7	International services
8	Transport
9	Caravans and houseboats
10	Gold
11	Bank notes
12	Drugs, medicines, aids for the handicapped etc.
13	Imports, exports etc.
14	*No longer in use*
15	Charities etc.
16	Clothing and footwear

Reduced rate supplies

Reduced rate goods and services are listed in Schedule 7A of the Value Added Tax Act 1994 which can be found in full here:

http://www.legislation.gov.uk/ukpga/1994/23/schedule/7A

The different reduced rated goods and services are:

Group Number	Goods/Services
1	Domestic fuel or power
2	Energy-saving materials, insulation
3	Heating equipment, security goods and gas supplied: grant-funded installation or connection
4	Women's sanitary products
5	Children's car seats
6	Residential conversions
7	Renovation and alteration of dwellings

Exempt supplies

If you supply exempt supplies, you do not charge VAT on your sales and you cannot register for VAT. A list of the exempt goods and services are listed in Schedule 9 of the Value Added Tax Act 1994 which can be found in full here:

http://www.legislation.gov.uk/ukpga/1994/23/schedule/9

The different exempt goods and services are:

Group Number	Goods/Services
1	Land
2	Insurance
3	Postal services
4	Betting, gaming and lotteries
5	Finance
6	Education
7	Health and welfare
8	Burial and cremation
9	Subscriptions to trade unions, professional and other public interest bodies
10	Sport, sports competitions and physical education
11	Works of art etc.
12	Fund raising events by charities and other qualifying bodies
13	Cultural services etc.
14	Supplies of goods where input tax cannot be recovered
15	Investment gold

Just because the goods and/or services you supply fall into a category above does not mean they are automatically zero rated, reduced rated or exempt. In fact, the rules can be quite complex and the links above details the conditions which should be met in order to qualify for that particular VAT rate.

For example, not all food is zero rated. Cold food, such as fresh meat or fruit and veg is zero rated, but a meal in a restaurant, while still food, is not zero rated as this is a supply in the course of catering.

If you believe your goods and services may fall into one of the categories above, you should read the detailed guidance to ensure it does qualify, or seek the advice of a professional who will be able to tell you what rate of VAT applies to your goods and services.

The difference between zero rated and exempt supplies

One common question from small business is "Why are there two rates of VAT which charge 0%" – the answer – there technically isn't!

Any zero rated goods and services do charge VAT, just at a 0% rate so that the actual VAT amount is £0.00. The goods or services are still VATable which means should your turnover from selling these items exceed the VAT Registration Threshold you should register.

Selling purely zero rated goods also means you can register for VAT and claim the Input VAT (the VAT you pay on the goods and services you buy) back from HMRC even though the VAT you charge your customers is zero. This will be explained more later.

Contrast this with exempt supplies, where you don't charge VAT, not even at 0%. If all your supplies are exempt, you cannot register for VAT, even if your turnover exceeds the VAT Registration Threshold. Therefore, the Input VAT you are charged is an additional cost to your business.

Standard rated supplies

If your goods or services do not fall into any of the three categories listed earlier (zero rated, reduced rated or exempt) they will be standard rated and if you are VAT registered you will charge VAT at the full rate on your sales.

Most businesses fall into this category.

CHAPTER 2: VAT Registration Requirements

VAT Registration Threshold

It is compulsory for you to Register for VAT in the UK you if your VAT taxable turnover (all supplies of goods and services that are not exempt) exceeds, or will exceed the VAT Registration Threshold. This threshold is £85,000 from 1 April 2017. This is usually uplifted in the Budget each year to take effect from 1 April.

There are two of tests business owners need to be aware of to determine if they should be registered for VAT. These tests are:

1. The next 30 day test
2. The previous 12 month test

The next 30 days test

If you expect your taxable turnover to exceed the VAT Registration Threshold in the next 30 days alone, you are required to register for VAT and charge VAT on your supplies immediately.

For example, say your business has been running for a few months, but has only had a taxable turnover of around £4,000 per month. However, after a few months a customer comes along and places an order for £100,000 and delivery will be made in two weeks' time.

You know once you have accepted the order that your taxable turnover will exceed the Registration Threshold within 30 days and you must therefore register immediately and you would charge VAT on that sale as well as all other sales moving forward.

If, however, the goods were to be sold and delivered over a four month period, your monthly turnover would only be £25,000. In no 30 day period do you expect turnover to exceed £85,000 and therefore the 30 day test does not apply.

The previous 12 month test

If the 'next 30 days test' does not apply then you just need to look at the 'previous 12 month test'. At the end of each calendar month, you would total up the sales for each of the 12 previous months and if this exceeds the VAT Registration Threshold you must register for VAT within 30 days of the end of the month in which the threshold was exceeded and charge VAT from the 1st day of the second month in which it was exceeded.

EXAMPLE

Mrs Smith and Mr Jones are both hairdressers who have been in business for many years, but have always been under the VAT Registration Threshold. On 1 January 2018 they both assess their taxable turnover for the previous 12 months and the figures are shown in the table below:

Month	Mrs Smith	Mr Jones
January 2017	£5,364	£6,169
February 2017	£5,564	£6,399
March 2017	£5,847	£6,724
April 2017	£5,317	£6,515
May 2017	£5,443	£6,259
June 2017	£6,295	£7,239
July 2017	£6,325	£7,274
August 2017	£5,941	£7,432
September 2017	£5,864	£7,244
October 2017	£5,741	£7,102
November 2017	£5,869	£7,749
December 2017	£7,813	£8,985
Total	**£71,383**	**£85,091**

Mrs Smith is clearly under the VAT Registration Threshold and therefore does not need to take any action. She will carry out the test again in February 2018 for the months of February 2017 to January 2018.

Mr Jones on the other hand has exceeded the VAT Registration Threshold (albeit by just £91) and he therefore has to Register for VAT within 30 days of 31 December 2017, being 30 January 2018. He will then charge VAT on his sales from the first day the second month after the threshold was exceeded, being 1 February 2018.

Applying for registration exception

If the value of your taxable supplies exceeds the VAT Registration Threshold you can apply for an exception from registration if you believe the value of your supplies in the next 12 months will not exceed the VAT de-registration threshold.

The current VAT de-registration threshold is £83,000.

For example, say Mr Jones from the earlier example has been opening his shop 6 days a week, but form 1 January 2018 he will close on a Monday which has historically been quite and only providing around 5% of turnover. The Monday customers are not expected to come to the salon on another day so his taxable turnover will reduce by 5% to £80,836. This is below the VAT de-registration threshold and he can therefore apply for exception.

REAL LIFE EXAMPLE – Applying for registration exception

Mrs Smith ran a small café which always traded below the VAT Registration Threshold. One summer the local council carried out major works to the road outside the café. This brought a lot of extra workmen to the area who used the café for meals and drinks throughout the day for the two month period they were working there.

This caused the café to exceed the VAT Registration Threshold based on the 'previous 12 month test' when this was checked after the second month of the roadworks.

Once the roadworks were complete, trading at the café fell back to the levels they were at roadworks commenced.

Mrs Smith applied to HMRC for exception from VAT Registration on the basis that the turnover only exceeded the threshold due to a one-off instance and in future the business will trade below the VAT deregistration threshold.

HMRC agreed and Mrs Smith did not need to register for VAT, which would have had a huge negative impact on her business as most of her sales were standard rated and she had very little input VAT to reclaim.

How to register

The easiest way to register for VAT is online using HMRC's website:

https://online.hmrc.gov.uk/registration/newbusiness/business-allowed

You can also apply by post be printing and completing Form VAT1:

https://www.gov.uk/government/publications/vat-application-for-registration-vat1

If your business is a partnership, you should also complete Form VAT2 to provide details of the partners:

https://www.gov.uk/government/publications/vat-partnership-details-vat2

CHAPTER 3: VAT schemes

As part of your VAT Registration Application, you will be asked if you want to apply for any VAT Schemes. These schemes can make taking care of VAT easier. The main schemes you can use are:

- Flat Rate Scheme
- Annual Accounting Scheme
- Cash Accounting Scheme

Flat Rate Scheme

The Flat Rate Scheme (FRS) is a scheme designed to make accounting for VAT simpler for small businesses. Under the FRS, businesses pay a flat amount of their VAT inclusive turnover to HMRC, but are restricted on the amount of input VAT they can reclaim.

The flat rate of VAT depends upon the type of goods and services the business sells. A list of flat rate categories is shown on Appendix One.

To be eligible to use the FRS the business' turnover must not exceed £150,000 (excluding VAT) when it applies to join the scheme.

You charge VAT as normal to your customers at the rate applicable to the goods or services you are supplying (standard, reduced or zero rated).

For example, John is a photographer and is VAT registered and uses the Flat Rate Scheme. He has calculated his turnover for his next VAT Return and his sales were £20,000 exclusive of VAT. His gross sales (including VAT) were £24,000.

The Flat Rate % for a photographer is 11%. John's liability is therefore £24,000 x 11% = £2,640. John collected £4,000 from his customers and the difference of £1,360 is to make up for John not being able to reclaim input VAT on his expenses.

When can input VAT be reclaimed?

When using the FRS input VAT can only be reclaimed when incurring capital expenditure and the total cost of the item including VAT exceeds £2,000. For example, say John the photographer purchased a new camera for £2,400, he can reclaim the £400 VAT he incurs on this as this is capital expenditure for more than £2,000.

Bad debts and FRS

If you are using the FRS and you incur a bad debt because a customer doesn't pay, you can reclaim the VAT charged to that customer in full.

For example, if included in John's sales was £1,200 (£1,000 + VAT) charged to Customer A, John would pay £132 to HMRC under the FRS (£1,200 x 11%). If Customer A does not pay, John can reclaim the full £200 VAT charged to that customer as a bad debt, not just the £132.

Applying for the Flat Rate Scheme

If registering for VAT online, you can apply to use the FRS as part of the application. Otherwise, you can complete Form VAT600FRS:

https://www.gov.uk/government/publications/vat-application-to-join-the-flat-rate-scheme-vat600frs

First year of VAT Registration and using the FRS

During your first year of VAT Registration you can receive a 1% discount on your normal flat rate %. This only applies during the first year of actual registration, not your first year of using the FRS. So, if you have been VAT Registered for many years, the 1% reduction will not apply.

When you MUST leave the Flat Rate Scheme

You must leave the FRS if your VAT-inclusive turnover:

- On the anniversary of joining the FRS exceeds £230,000 in the previous 12 months or you expect to in the next 12 months;
- You expect it to exceed £230,000 in the next 30 days alone

Limited cost trader under the Flat Rate Scheme

On 1 April 2017 H M Revenue & Customs made a major change to the VAT Flat Rate Scheme by introducing a new rate for 'limited cost traders'. The rate is 16.5%. If this rate applies, for every £20.00 you collect in VAT from your customers when using the FRS you pay HMRC £19.80. It is no longer considered viable for any person who falls into this category to use the FRS.

The maximum gain a limited cost trader can make each year would be:

VAT charged to customers on maximum sales	
£230,000 x 1/6	£38,333
VAT payable to HMRC under the Flat Rate Scheme	
£230,000 x 16.5%	£37,950
Difference	£383

The business would only need to have input VAT on its purchases and expenses of £383 per annum in order to be better off under the normal accounting scheme.

What is a limited cost trader?

A limited cost trader is someone whose VAT-inclusive expenditure on **goods** is less £1,000 per annum (pro-rata if the VAT period is less than a year) or less than 2% of their VAT inclusive-turnover in the VAT period if the expenditure on goods is greater than £1,000.

What are goods?

Goods for the purpose of determining if you are a limited cost trader excludes:capital expenditure

- food and drink for consumption of the business or its employees
- vehicles, vehicles parts and vehicle fuel (except where the business is one which carries out transport services).

Annual Accounting Scheme

Normally, business will submit a VAT Return every three months. Under the Annual Accounting Scheme (AAS), a Return will only be submitted once a year, but they will pay VAT every month or quarter. The payment will be an installment figure based on the estimated liability for the year.

To be eligible to join the AAS, the businesses taxable turnover must not exceed £1.35 million, excluding VAT.

You cannot use the scheme if you have left the Annual Accounting Scheme in the last 12 months, if your business is part of a VAT registered group of companies, if you're insolvent or if you are not up to date with your VAT Returns or payments.

VAT Return under AAS

Business who use the AAS have a 12 month VAT period, rather than the normal 3 month period. The VAT Return must be submitted within two months of the end of the 12 month period.

VAT payments under AAS

Under the AAS you will either make VAT payments monthly or quarterly.

If you make monthly payments, you will make a payment of 10% of your estimated annual liability in months 4 to 12. You will then make a balancing payment within 2 months after month 12 to settle the full liability for the year, or claim a refund if you have paid too much in the 9 installments.

If you make quarterly payments, you will make a payment of 25% of your estimated annual liability in months 4, 7 and 10. You will then make a balancing payment within 2 months after month 12 to settle the full liability for the year, or claim a refund if you have paid too much in the 9 installments.

Example

John is VAT Registered and uses the Annual Accounting Scheme. His year end is 31 March and for the year ended 31 March 2017 his estimated VAT liability is £12,000.

During the months of July 2016 to March 2017, John makes 9 monthly payments on account of £1,200. John completes his VAT Return by 31 May 2017 and calculates his actual VAT liability was £13,350. He must therefore pay the balance of £2,550 by 31 May 2017.

When you MUST leave the Annual Accounting Scheme

You must leave the AAS if:

- You VATable turnover exceeds (or is likely to exceed) £1.6 million at the end of the annual accounting year.
- You are no longer eligible (e.g. your business becomes part of a VAT registered group)

Applying for the Annual Accounting Scheme

If registering for VAT online, you can apply to use the AAS as part of the application. Otherwise, you can complete Form VAT600AA:

https://www.gov.uk/government/publications/vat-application-to-join-the-annual-accounting-scheme-vat600aa

If you wish to apply for the Flat Rate and Annual Accounting Schemes at the same time, you can complete Form VAT600AA/FRS:

https://www.gov.uk/government/publications/vat-application-to-join-the-annual-accounting-and-flat-rate-scheme-vat600aafrs

Cash Accounting Scheme

The normal rules for accounting for VAT payable to HMRC on sales, and reclaimable from HMRC on purchases and expenses, is determined by the tax point (generally, the date on the invoice).

However, if your taxable turnover is £1.35 million or less, you can use the Cash Accounting Scheme (CAS). You do not need to apply to HMRC to use the CAS, so you can start to use the scheme at any point as long as you are eligible as per the taxable turnover rule above.

Under the CAS you:

- Pay VAT over to HMRC on your sales in the quarter when your customer actually pays you
- Reclaim VAT on your purchases and expenses in the quarter when you pay your supplier

The CAS can provide a cash flow advantage as you don't need to pay the VAT on your sales until you have actually received the money from your customer. This can be helpful where you provide extended credit to your customers.

However, you also cannot claim the VAT on your purchases and expenses until you have actually paid for them, so if you take a long time to pay your suppliers you will have to wait to get the credit for the VAT you have been charged.

If your supplies are zero rated using the CAS will delay getting your VAT refunds from HMRC. Therefore, business with zero rated supplies (or mainly zero rated supplied) should not use the Cash Accounting Scheme.

CHAPTER 4: What happens after registration

Once you are Registered for VAT you must start to charge VAT on your sales from the date of registration, which will be shown on your VAT Registration Certificate. The rate of VAT you charge will be determined by the actual goods or services you are selling as explained in chapter one.

You will need to complete a VAT Return, usually every three months. A VAT Return consists of 9 boxes of information about your sales, purchases and expenses and VAT thereon and the overall liability or refund of VAT due for the period.

VAT Returns must be filed online and are due by the 7th of the second month following the end of the period. For example, the VAT Return for the period ended 30 June 2017 is due for filing by 7 August 2017. Payment is due at the same time, however, if you pay by direct debit, payment will be collected 3 working days after the filing deadline, which will be around 10th to 12th of the month depending upon weekends and bank holidays.

Regular repayments

If you expect to receive regular VAT repayments (i.e. the VAT you incur regularly exceeds the VAT you collect on your sales, because your sales are zero rated for example) then you can apply to submit your VAT Returns on a monthly basis rather than a quarterly basis.

Whilst this will mean more paperwork, it also means you get your VAT repayments on a monthly basis too which will help improve your business' cash flow.

CHAPTER 5: When is registering for VAT beneficial even if not compulsory

The are some scenarios where registering for VAT can benefit a business, even if it is not legally required to do so (because the taxable supplies made by the business are below the VAT Registration Threshold).

Example A – Zero Rated Goods and Services Supplied (REAL LIFE)

Tina sells fruit and veg to the general public with annual sales of around £50,000. There is therefore no requirement for Tina to be VAT Registered. However, Tina's sales are zero rated as they are food as described by Group 1 of Schedule 8 of VATA 1994 (see Chapter 1).

Therefore, if Tina became VAT Registered, her prices wouldn't change as she would charge VAT at 0%, but she would be able to claim back the VAT she is charged on her expenses.

Tina had purchased a van and incurs ongoing motor expenses as well as incurring VAT on expenses such as telephone, a business website and uniforms. Tina can reclaim all of this input VAT back form HMRC which is additional profit for her business.

In this example, Tina got a one off repayment of £2,500 relating to VAT on the purchase of the business van and capital items and gets regular repayments of £700 - £1,200 per annum which is all additional profit for the business.

Example B – Customers are other VAT Registered Businesses (REAL LIFE)

David is a handyman whose customers are all other business which are VAT registered. David's taxable supplies are around £60,000 and his cost of sales, including VAT, is around 40% of sales. David also has a van, tools, business telephone and other overheads on which he incurs VAT.

David could register for VAT and whilst he would have to add 20% VAT onto his sales price, his customers won't be concerned by this as they will be able to reclaim this on their own VAT Returns. The only effect on David's customers is a small cash flow disadvantage as they will pay David an additional 20% up to three months before being able to reclaim this form HMRC.

David can reclaim the VAT he incurs on the purchase of materials, tools and other expenses he incurs resulting in more profit for his business without costing his customers more.

In this scenario, David actually increased his annual profit by £5,000 - £7,000 just by being able to reclaim the input VAT he was being charged.

Example C – Courier working for various companies (REAL LIFE)

Steve works as a self-employed courier. His taxable turnover is £90,000 per annum and he charges £18,000 VAT to his various customers throughout the year.

Whilst Steve is VAT registered, his costs are fairly static as he usually works in one area so his fuel costs do not change dramatically when his turnover does.

Under the normal VAT rules, Steve would pay the £18,000 VAT to HMRC and claim around £5,000 input VAT from HMRC, so a net payment of £13,000 each year.

However, Steve applied to use the Flat Rate Scheme, and pays over 10% of his VAT-inclusive turnover to HMRC: £108,000 x 10% = £10,800. Compared to the amount paid under the normal VAT method of £13,000 this is an additional £2,200 profit per annum.

CHAPTER 6: Avoid VAT Registration?

This is NOT as you are thinking, and I am certainly not telling you to not register if you meet the requirements to register, but there are some circumstances where it may be beneficial to take on less work and be able to make more money by avoiding being VAT registered.

Say you operate a shop which has weekly takings of £1,650. If you opened for 52 weeks of the year, your annual turnover would be £85,800, just over the registration threshold. Assuming you couldn't pass on the 20% VAT to your customers so would have to incur this cost yourself, this would be VAT on sales of £85,800 x 1/6 = £14,300.

Being VAT registered, you would be able to reclaim the VAT you have suffered, but this is likely to be less than the output VAT and you would therefore be out of pocket.

If instead, you closed the shop for 2 weeks of the year, your taxable turnover would be £1,650 x 50 = £82,500 which is under the VAT threshold. You would lose out on £3,300 worth of sales, but you would still be better off unless the input VAT you suffer on your costs is greater than £11,000 (£14,300 - £3,300).

Customers who aren't VAT Registered

Usually you will find that if you are a small business, becoming VAT Registered overnight will increase your prices by 20% and could put off a lot of your customers – after all who likes a 20% price increase!

Therefore, you may find it difficult to deal with becoming VAT registered and could lose some customers. Being on the borderline presents a difficult decision for you to make, do you get on with business and become VAT registered, increase prices and potentially upsetting customers, or do you turn down some work to stay under the Threshold and avoid the additional paperwork and hassle? This is a decision only you can make and you need to weigh up the ease of not being VAT registered, and potential losses if price increases can't be passed onto customers, with the potential growth you would be giving up.

If you do become VAT registered, you may have room to maneuver over your price increase whilst still making more profit.

For example, Lucy supplies furniture to private individuals and her turnover has just exceeded the VAT Registration Threshold and is £86,000 per annum. Business is expected to continue at a similar level, and Lucy can get away with a bit of a price increase but not a full 20% increase.

Lucy incurs costs of 60% (inclusive of VAT) on her sales, being £51,600 (£8,600 VAT).

Lucy could close for a week or two to reduce her turnover to £80,000, or become VAT Registered and pass 10% of the price increase to her customers (half the VAT). The results would be:

	Not VAT Registered	**VAT Registered**	Notes
Sales	£80,000	£94,600	1
Output VAT	£0	£15,767	2
Net turnover (A)	**£80,000**	**£78,833**	
Cost of sales	£48,000	£51,600	3
Input VAT reclaimable	£0	£8,600	4
Net cost of sales (B)	**£48,000**	**£43,000**	
Gross profit (A – B)	**£32,000**	**£35,833**	

Note – Lucy would also be able to reclaim the VAT on her overheads increasing her profit even further.

[1] - £86,000 x 110%

[2] - £94,600 x 1/6

[3] - £86,000 x 60% (based on turnover before cost increase)

[4] - £51,600 x 1/6

Appendix 1 – Flat Rate Categories

Type of business	Current VAT flat rate (%)
Accountancy or book-keeping	14.5
Advertising	11.0
Agricultural services	11.0
Any other activity not listed elsewhere	12.0
Architect, civil and structural engineer or surveyor	14.5
Boarding or care of animals	12.0
Business services not listed elsewhere	12.0
Catering services including restaurants and takeaways	12.5
Computer and IT consultancy or data processing	14.5
Computer repair services	10.5
Entertainment or journalism	12.5
Estate agency or property management services	12.0
Farming or agriculture not listed elsewhere	6.5
Film, radio, television or video production	13.0
Financial services	13.5
Forestry or fishing	10.5
General building or construction services*	9.5
Hairdressing or other beauty treatment services	13.0
Hiring or renting goods	9.5
Hotel or accommodation	10.5
Investigation or security	12.0
Labour-only building or construction services*	14.5
Laundry or dry-cleaning services	12.0
Lawyer or legal services	14.5
Library, archive, museum or other cultural activity	9.5
Management consultancy	14.0
Manufacturing fabricated metal products	10.5
Manufacturing food	9.0

Manufacturing not listed elsewhere	9.5
Manufacturing yarn, textiles or clothing	9.0
Membership organisation	8.0
Mining or quarrying	10.0
Packaging	9.0
Photography	11.0
Post offices	5.0
Printing	8.5
Publishing	11.0
Pubs	6.5
Real estate activity not listed elsewhere	14.0
Repairing personal or household goods	10.0
Repairing vehicles	8.5
Retailing food, confectionery, tobacco, newspapers or children's clothing	4.0
Retailing pharmaceuticals, medical goods, cosmetics or toiletries	8.0
Retailing not listed elsewhere	7.5
Retailing vehicles or fuel	6.5
Secretarial services	13.0
Social work	11.0
Sport or recreation	8.5
Transport or storage, including couriers, freight, removals and taxis	10.0
Travel agency	10.5
Veterinary medicine	11.0
Wholesaling agricultural products	8.0
Wholesaling food	7.5
Wholesaling not listed elsewhere	8.5

*'Labour-only building or construction services' means building services where the value of the materials supplied is less than 10% of the turnover for those services. If more than this amount, the business is classed as 'General building or construction services'.

GLOSSARY

Annual Accounting Scheme

A simplified scheme for accounting for VAT payable to HMRC by completing only one VAT Return a year.

Bad Debt

A sale to a customer on credit which will not be paid

Cash Accounting Scheme

A scheme to allow you to account for VAT on your VAT Return on a basis of cash receipts and payments.

Deregistration Threshold

The level of taxable supplies which determines if a business can deregister for VAT or apply for Exception, currently £83,000.

Exception

A VAT Exception Application can be made if your taxable supplies have exceeded the Registration Threshold but you expect them to be below the Deregistration Threshold in the next 12 months.

Exempt Services

Services on which VAT is not charged.

Flat Rate Scheme

A simplified scheme for accounting for VAT payable to HMRC by applying a flat % to your VAT inclusive turnover.

HMRC

H M Revenue & Customs - the government department responsible for administration of VAT.

Input VAT

VAT incurred by a business on the purchase of goods and services.

Output VAT

VAT charged by a business on its sales of goods and services.

Reduced Rated

A lower rate of VAT on certain goods and services, currently 5%.

Registration Threshold

The level of taxable supplies which if a business exceeds it is required to be VAT registered, currently £85,000.

Standard Rated

The main rate of VAT, currently 20%.

Taxable Turnover

The sales value of your goods and services which are standard rated, reduced rated and zero rated.

VAT

Value Added Tax - a tax on the sale of goods and services.

VAT Return

A VAT Return consists of 9 boxes of figures to report to HMRC and calculate VAT payable or refundable.

VATA 1994

Value Added Tax Act 1994 - the law concerning VAT.

Zero Rated

A zero rate of VAT on certain goods and services.

Printed in Great Britain
by Amazon

20458877R00020